ANKYLOSAURUS
A First Look

JERI RANCH

GRL Consultant, Diane Craig, Certified Literacy Specialist

Lerner Publications ◆ Minneapolis

Educator Toolbox

Reading books is a great way for kids to express what they're interested in. Before reading this title, ask the reader these questions:

> What do you think this book is about? Look at the cover for clues.

> What do you already know about this dinosaur?

> What do you want to learn about this dinosaur?

Let's Read Together

Encourage the reader to use the pictures to understand the text.

Point out when the reader successfully sounds out a word.

Praise the reader for recognizing sight words such as *it* and *was*.

TABLE OF CONTENTS

Ankylosaurus

Ankylosaurus is a kind of dinosaur. It lived 66 million years ago.

Ankylosaurus
ang-kull-oh-SOAR-us

The dinosaur was large.
It was heavier than
a hippo.

hippo

Plates covered its back.
The plates were made of bone.

They helped keep
the dinosaur safe.

How would bony plates
keep a dinosaur safe?

It had a beak.
It had small teeth.

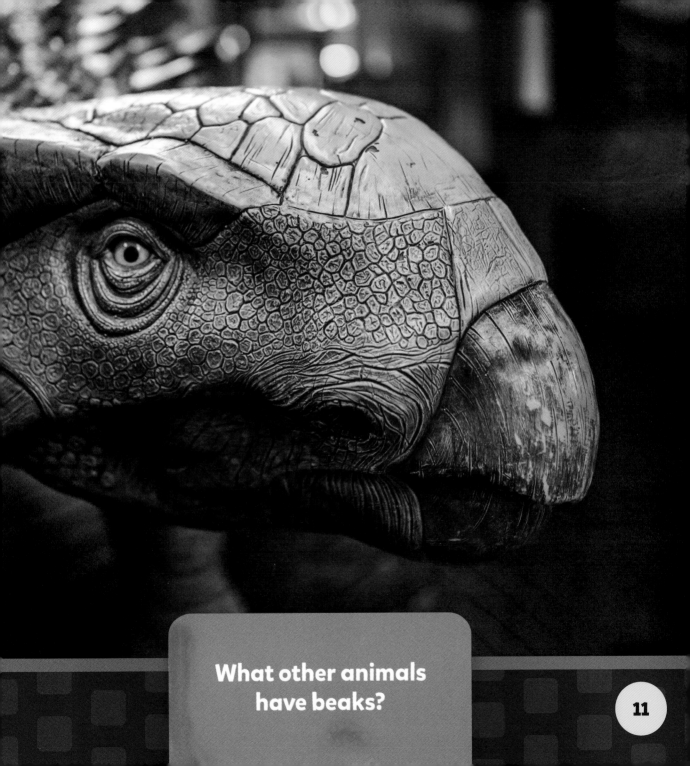

What other animals have beaks?

It had a long tail.
A heavy club was on the end.
The dinosaur used it to fight.

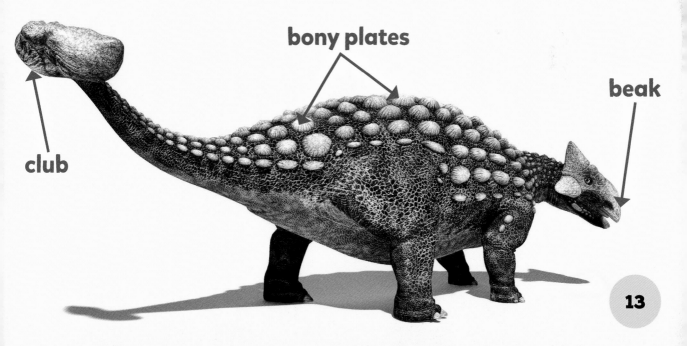

bony plates

beak

club

It lived in warm areas.
There were many trees.

It ate plants.

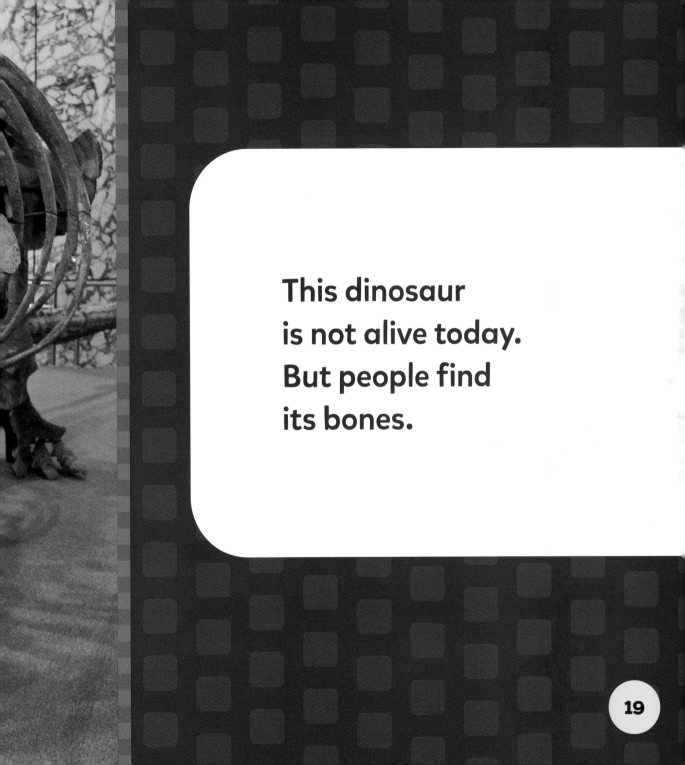

This dinosaur
is not alive today.
But people find
its bones.

Bones help us learn
about this dinosaur.

You Connect!

What is something you like about this dinosaur?

What else is as big as this dinosaur?

What other dinosaurs do you know about?

STEM Snapshot

Encourage students to think and ask questions like scientists. Ask the reader:

What is something you learned about this dinosaur?

What is something you noticed in the pictures of the dinosaur?

What is something you still don't know about this dinosaur?

Photo Glossary

Learn More

Carr, Aaron. *Ankylosaurus*. New York: AV2, 2022.

Radley, Gail. *Ankylosaurus*. Mankato, MN: Black Rabbit Books, 2021.

Sabelko, Rebecca. *Ankylosaurus*. Minneapolis: Bellwether Media, 2020.

Index

Photo Acknowledgments

The images in this book are used with the permission of: © Daniel Eskridge/Shutterstock Images, pp. 4–5, 6–7, 9, 12, 14–15, 23 (plates); © Rudi Hulshof/Shutterstock Images, pp. 7, 23 (hippo); © Warpaint/Shutterstock Images, p. 8; © Rachelle Van De Kamp/Shutterstock Images, pp. 10–11, 23 (beak); © Matis75/Shutterstock Images, p. 13; © Pav-Pro Photography Ltd/Shutterstock Images, pp. 16–17; © Gary Todd/Wikimedia Commons, pp. 18–19, 23 (bones); © Gary Todd/Flickr, p. 20.

Cover Photograph: © Daniel Eskridge/Shutterstock Images

Design Elements: © Mighty Media, Inc.

Lerner Publications Company
An imprint of Lerner Publishing Group, Inc.
241 First Avenue North
Minneapolis, MN 55401 USA

For reading levels and more information, look up this title at www.lernerbooks.com.

Main body text set in Mikado a Medium.
Typeface provided by Hannes von Doehren.

Library of Congress Cataloging-in-Publication Data

Names: Ranch, Jeri, author.
Title: Ankylosaurus : a first look / Jeri Ranch.
Description: Minneapolis : Lerner Publications, [2024] | Series: Read about dinosaurs (Read for a better world) | Includes bibliographical references and index. | Audience: Ages 5–8 | Audience: Grades K–1 | Summary: "Young readers will delight in learning about the massive, armored Ankylosaurus. Carefully leveled text and full-color images help these prehistoric creatures come to life"—Provided by publisher.
Identifiers: LCCN 2022033289 (print) | LCCN 2022033290 (ebook) | ISBN 9781728491332 (library binding) | ISBN 9798765603451 (paperback) | ISBN 9781728499147 (ebook)
Subjects: LCSH: Ankylosaurus—Juvenile literature. | Dinosaurs—Juvenile literature.
Classification: LCC QE862.O65 R3597 2024 (print) | LCC QE862.O65 (ebook) | DDC 567.915—dc23/eng20221208

LC record available at https://lccn.loc.gov/2022033289
LC ebook record available at https://lccn.loc.gov/2022033290

Manufactured in the United States of America
2-1009744-51082-5/31/2023